Paris

Véronique Laflèche

Publishing Director: Jean-Paul Manzo
Text: Véronique Laflèche
Translation: Mike Darton
Publishing assistant: Vanessa Basille
Design and layout : Cédric Pontes
Cover and jacket : Cédric Pontes

We are very grateful to the Saint-Séverin parish, Mrs Brethé of the 18th *arrondissement*'s
mayor's office and Mr Denis Pasquier of the City of Science and Industry for their kind
cooperation.
© Parkstone Press Ltd, New York, USA, 2002
ISBN 1 85995 845 1
Printed and bound in Hong Kong

Photograph Credits:
© Klaus H. Carl : ill.11, 13, 14, 17, 18, 22, 23, 24, 25, 28, 29, 31, 32, 33, 34, 35, 36, 37, 41,
    42, 43, 45, 51, 56, 57, 62, 63, 64, 65, 66, 67, 68, 70, 71, 72, 73, 74, 79, 84, 86, 88, 91, 93,
    94, 100, 101, 102, 103, 104, 107, 108, 109, 111, 112, 113, 114.
© D. Rocha : ill. 26, 46, 47, 58.
© CSI/Arnaud Le Grain : ill. 119, 120.
© Alain Lonchampt/Centre des Monuments Nationaux, Paris : ill. 75.
© Jean-Marc Charles/Centre des Monuments Nationaux, Paris : ill.90.
© Patrick Müller/Centre des Monuments Nationaux, Paris : ill. 69.
© Paroisse St Séverin : ill. 39, 40.
© ND Viollet : ill. 6, 7, 9, 10.
© J.Valliot : ill. 12, 16, 19, 20, 21, 27, 44, 48, 50, 59, 60, 61, 76, 77, 78, 80, 81, 83, 85, 87, 89,
    95, 96, 97, 98, 99, 106, 110, 115.
© J. Mahu : ill. 15, 30, 38,52,53, 54, 55, 92.
© Pictures Colour Library : ill. 105, 121.
© Comité des Fêtes et d'Action Sociale du 18e arrondissement/Thierry Nectoux : ill. 116.
© Comité des Fêtes et d'Action Sociale du 18e arrondissement/ Bernard Daunas : ill. 117, 118.

Paris

Véronique Laflèche

Table of Contents

INTRODUCTION

Paris has its own special atmosphere – an atmosphere that every day draws hundreds of thousands of visitors to it from all over the world. No one can be lukewarm about Paris. Of mythical status, the city is so disarmingly seductive that everyone who leaves it always means to return.

The centre of the city bears ample evidence of a past rich in history – a past that is nonetheless perfectly integrated into an urban area in active and constant evolution.

Most radiant of cities, most romantic of cities, Paris is ever ready to lend itself to the heady emotions of admirers who revel in its wonders.

JUST A LITTLE HISTORY . . .

Recent excavations in the area of Bercy have brought to light a number of small boats dating from the 5th millennium BC. Much later, in the 5th century BC, the Celtic tribe that was to be known to the Romans as the *Parisii* occupied the centre of the Paris Basin, a fertile plain irrigated by the River Seine and by several other rivers. Their main settlement was an island in the middle of the southern branch of the Seine – the island now called the Île de la Cité. It was a site chosen for the protection afforded by surrounding hills, but that protection was utterly futile in the face of the barbarian hordes that later raged across the land.

In 52 BC the Romans turfed out the *Parisii* and took over the Île. The ensuing Gallo-Roman period lasted for close to three centuries. It was a time of peace – the enforced Pax Romana –, which for the township was also a time of prosperity. The Roman administrative authorities were located on the Île de la Cité, while on the Left Bank stood the forum, an amphitheatre, another theatre, and the public baths. The present-day Rue Saint-Jacques corresponds to an ancient Gallo-Roman trackway linking other settlements to the north and south.

The area then became subject to attacks by Germanic barbarians, and a protective embankment was built around the Cité. At the beginning of the 4th century AD, the town – known contemporarily as Lutetia – began instead to be called by the name of its original inhabitants, the *civitas Parisiorum* ('the city of the *Parisii*'), from which Paris takes its modern name.

1- April 14th, 1900; inauguration of the *Exposition universelle* (World's fair).

6

Led by Attila, the Huns marched on Paris in 451, but apparently through the prayers of St Genevieve (who thereafter became a patron saint of Paris) were diverted away from the city before they actually got there. In 508 the Merovingian King Clovis made Paris his capital. Many great ecclesiastical buildings – including St Stephen's cathedral (later to become Notre-Dame) on the Île de la Cité, the basilica of St Denis (Sacré-Cœur) and various other foundations – were constructed, testimony to tremendous religious fervour over the following 500 years; testimony too to enormous economic growth, proof of which is the establishment there of the mint. The city's population eventually reached 15,000.

Between the 11th and the 13th centuries Paris underwent considerable expansion during something of a Golden Age. After the Cité and the Left Bank, it was the turn of the Right Bank of the river to be developed. The area became the business and financial quarter – as it still is today – in which Jewish and Lombard businessmen were prominent. The increase of water traffic on the river required the development also of port facilities at the Grève, while food supplies for the city were channelled through Les Halles. Marshy areas were drained and brought under cultivation – although the district is still known as the Marais ('Marsh').

2- The peristyle of the Grand Palais.

During the Middle Ages, the population of Paris topped 50,000. King Philip II Augustus, at the end of the 12th century, enhanced the city's defensive ramparts on both Banks, and set up the fortress that was the Louvre (which he called 'our tower'). He reorganized the wharves and jetties to accommodate the commercial upsurge on the Seine, and began paving the more frequented streets of Paris. However there was no attempt at hygiene. Raw sewage tossed unceremoniously into the street was removed only by the ordinary rainwater drainage system, making transport on both road and river hazardous in many ways. It was the same all through the 13th century – indeed, in some areas of the capital it was the same right up until the 19th century. The Seine was horribly polluted. Drinking water therefore posed another problem: natural springs had to have pipes fitted to them, wells had to be dug, channelling systems (including aqueducts) had to be constructed, so that the inhabitants could drink safely.

3- The Champs-de-Mars.

4- The Pont Alexandre-III.

Paris was governed by a representative of the Crown, the Provost, whose official residence was the Châtelet, and who was in charge of the judiciary. In addition, the civic guild of rivertraders elected their own community representative. Together, these two municipal officers constituted the beginnings of civic authority in Paris. Their official seal – featuring a boat and the motto *Fluctuat nec mergitur* ('It floats and is not submerged') – remains part of the city's heraldic coat of arms.

On the Île de la Cité, a new cathedral church began to rise as a replacement for the church of St Stephen. It was eventually to become Notre-Dame, but was the first inspiration of Bishop Maurice de Sully in 1163. By 1245 King Louis IX had added the splendidly Gothic Sainte-Chapelle.

The medieval era was marked by the high standards of ecclesiastical learning particularly evident in abbeys and clerical schools, among which was the cathedral school of Notre-Dame. In the 12th century, the schools of the Cité moved on to the Left Bank and was organized into a university, which, from the 13th century, was to be influential all over Europe. To accommodate the scholars and their lecturers, residential colleges were constructed in which lectures could be delivered to the students who lived on the premises. Robert de Sorbon founded such a college in 1253 – from which the name Sorbonne derives. In the 21st century the area is still mostly peopled with university students and is still called the Latin Quarter.

Paris prospered and expanded: soon there were 200,000 citizens. It became the economic, cultural and intellectual capital – but many very serious difficulties then intervened. The Hundred Years' War, the Black Death (1348–1349), poverty, famine, icy winters and swinging taxes all caused civil unrest. An uprising was led by the merchant guildsman Etienne Marcel, but it was crushed and he was killed in 1358. A revolt finally succeeded in 1418, but led to occupation of the city by Burgundians. Joan of Arc then failed to deliver Paris from Burgundian and English dominance (1429) and was burned at the stake for her pains (1431), although she inspired a new movement for national unity.

Paris was thus depleted of about half its population; those who remained suffered severe poverty. Yet things got even worse. In the time of Charles VII, the royal court moved to Touraine, and although some administrative reorganization took place in Paris, it was the Val de Loire that benefited most. This is where first vestiges of the forthcoming Renaissance were already appearing.

The onset of the Renaissance was given a boost by the invention of the printing press during the 15th century, which rendered the laborious hand copying used up till now unnecessary" In 1530, Francis I founded the College of the King's Lectors (later the Collège de France), and in 1570 Charles IX founded the first Académie Française.

It was Francis I who decided that Paris should once again act as the seat of royalty in France, although it was his successor Henry II who made a ceremonial entrance into the capital in 1549, to take up residence in the Louvre.

5- General view of Paris.

The 16th century saw the population of Paris grow to around 350,000 inhabitants – which itself caused problems of accommodation and of personal security. In spite of the increase in the number of paved roads, the imposition of systems to regularly collect or clear sewage, as well as an initial attempt to install public street lighting, everyday life in Paris was harsh – drinking-water was still in short and uncertain supply.

Religious strife between Catholics and the Protestant Huguenots came to a head in the terrible slaughter of the Huguenots that came to be known as the St Bartholomew's Day Massacre, at the end of August 1572.

It was not until the end of the century and the readmission to Paris of King Henry IV after he had converted to Catholicism that the capital really began to experience more tranquil times.

It was Henry who would leave his mark on the district of the Marais, giving it much of the appearance it has today, with its fine and typically French *hôtels*. He designed the Place Royale (now the Place des Vosges), the Place Dauphine, and relaid out the Île Saint-Louis. Bridges – including the Pont-Neuf – were built to link the islands with the two Banks. Transport and communications were vastly improved. The Faubourg (suburb) Saint-Germain benefited greatly from it, and expanded in its turn.

Not far from the Tuileries, laid out a generation before by Catherine de Médicis, Cardinal Richelieu – one of Louis XIII's ministers – constructed the Palais-Cardinal, which he bequeathed to the Crown at his death. It was later to become the Palais-Royal.

Serious economic problems then bedevilled the royal court. Subsequent high levels of taxation poisoned relations between the court and parliament to the extent that there was some civil unrest and the occasional putting up of barricades. However the young Louis XIV managed, in time, to impose his authority. Technically resident in the Louvre, he spent most of his time in Versailles from 1671. It was his intention to expand on Louis XIII's territory and modernize the city to his own aesthetic tastes. There was to be nighttime street lighting with oil lanterns. The distribution of drinking water was to be upgraded. A fire brigade and a general hospital were to be established, as was a public transportation system. The Place des Victoires and the Place de Louis-le-Grand (now the Place Vendôme) bear witness to the power and the glory of Louis XIV, rightly known then and since as 'the Sun King'.

From the 16th century on, ladies of culture and refinement in Paris were accustomed to receiving the intelligentsia – notably philosophers and artists – in their literary *salons*. By the 18th century, such *salons* were the showpieces of French civilization and the envy of Europe. Foreigners loved to be invited. Casanova, in the 1770s, certainly did. It was in such surroundings (and in more recent institutions like cafés) that the mix and flow of new ideas could be presented which in time would inspire the French Revolution.

A nauseating stench unimaginable to a Parisian of the 21st century plagued the capital. Nonetheless, everyday living conditions gradually got better. The revised layout of the Place Louis-XV (today the Place de la Concorde) enabled the convergence of two major directional routes and the consequent siting of what is now surely the most beautiful avenue in the world: the Champs Elysées. In around the 1770s Philippe, Duke of Orléans, converted the gardens of the Palais-Royal into a profit-making enterprise, installing wooden galleries.

At the end of the 18th century, a circular wall was built around Paris. Known as the wall of the Farmers-General (senior tax officials), it enclosed the area subject to import duties (*octrois*) and was unpopular, to say the least, with Parisians. In fact, taxes together with political and economic crises, famine, and widespread poverty were sorely trying the people's patience. Rioting broke out. The storming of the Bastille prison by a howling mob took place on July 14, 1789 – a day now celebrated as a national holiday in France.

The Terror then raged in Paris. The king was guillotined in the Place de la Concorde on January 21, 1793, followed by Queen Marie-Antoinette on October 16th, after several terrifying weeks in the Conciergerie. Nearly 3,000 people were executed in two years. Revolutionary Paris thought nothing of stealing the prized possessions of the Church or of vandalising ecclesiastical buildings, or of looting and torching in general, without fear of consequences in this life or the next.

General Napoleon Bonaparte became the Emperor Napoleon I on December 2, 1804, following his successful campaigns of war across Europe. His many victories in battle had, among other things, furnished the Louvre with a host of priceless works of art. But then came the defeats.

6- The Place de la Bastille and the July Column. This column, measuring 50.52 m in height, dates back to 1883 and commemorates the death of the 504 victims of the July Revolution. Each one of their names is engraved on its bronze shaft.

7- The Arc de Triomphe and the Avenue des Champs Elysées in 1900.

Often absent from Paris on his military adventures, Napoleon determined that the city should become the most beautiful in the world. After a decade of demolition, he oversaw the beginning of important reconstruction work intended to improve the living conditions of all Parisians. There was very little money to spare; yet what he did manage to get done is remarkable, including the arcades of the Rue de Rivoli, some new bridges, the Place de la Bastille and the canal Bassin de la Villette. He also ordered the erection of the triumphal arches of the Etoile and of the Carrousel.

Paris experienced days of serious civil unrest in 1830, and then again in 1848. From 1830, the city underwent a process of transformation through rapid industrialization. A network of rail services was inaugurated, and many stations built (1835–1848).

The 19th century was another era of change for the capital. Water was piped into the houses, drains were laid that really did what they were supposed to, communal transportation systems forked in all directions, gas lighting became widespread. By 1850, the city could count around one million inhabitants. Baron Georges Haussmann – Prefect of the Seine under Emperor Napoleon III for nigh on twenty years (1853–1870) – completely changed the look of Paris by demolishing swathes of sub-standard housing to build great arterial thoroughfares from which fine views of the city were visible. Haussman has rightly been described as 'the creator of modern Paris'. At the same time he could be said to have broken up the city's overall unity. It was in 1860 that Paris was divided into 20 *arrondissements*.

Society in 19th-century Paris was riddled with inequalities. On the one hand were the working-class poor, subject to innumerable diseases and disorders (notably cholera and tuberculosis) and largely hooked on alcohol. On the other was the *bourgeoisie* – actively seeking amusing (and preferably licentious) ways to spend all its money.

The second half of the 19th century was the era of the great *expositions universelles*, the 'World's Fairs', of fashionable society in unprecedented turmoil, and of the creation of the large department stores that sounded the death-knell of the 'pavement arcades', typically Parisian commercial and artistic meeting-places since the beginning of the century.

In 1870 Paris was besieged by German forces, to which it capitula-ted on March 1, 1871. Its disillusioned citizens reacted with riots and arson attacks. The Hôtel de Ville, the Palais de Justice, the Tuileries, the Palais-Royal and various other prominent premises were destroyed. The Paris Commune saw thousands of fatalities, and for some years the city was no longer capital of the country. Political life was poisoned by scandals and disgrace (the Dreyfus affair, Panama, etc.).

Yet Paris was to emerge at the end of the 19th century, perhaps surprisingly, with much to be proud of – the Eiffel Tower, the metro, electrically powered trams, and the motorcar.

The first years of the 20th century are those known collectively in French as the *Belle Epoque*, a time renowned for the vigor of its cultural and artistic prowess. It was also a time in which the art-inspired architect Hector Guimard put his own imprint on Paris by imposing Art Nouveau forms (involving curves, and asymmetrical and exaggerated details) in place of the former coldly austere style of Baron Haussmann. His sensuous and harmonious style lit a flame that continued to burn, for architects after him (Le Corbusier, Mallet-Stevens and others) tended to concentrate on cubic and rhomboid shapes. Guimard is celebrated for his subway entrances, works of acknowledged genius. French painting meanwhile displayed its explosive vitality in the works of the Impressionists and the Fauves. Artists congregated mostly in the 'villages' of first Montmartre and then Montparnasse. Literature flourished. The *ballets russes* under Diaghilev also saw worldwide fame and success.

The aftermath in Paris of the First World War (1914–1918) was a regrettable state of lethargy that nullified the enthusiasm for moderni-zation originally inculcated by Baron Haussmann. Now with nearly three million citizens, Paris experienced a serious shortage of living accommo-dation leading to misery for many – and this at exactly the same time (the interwar years) as a rich minority was swanning around in insouciant opulence.

The Second World War (for the French, 1939–1944) to many Parisians was something of a 'phoney war'. Life went on, albeit at a slower pace, with rationing-slips, bribery and corruption, black marketeering, the Resistance and its activities, and the persecution of the Jews. The capital was liberated from the Germans on August 25, 1944, without having suffered the slightest damage. To pick itself up after such years of depression, however, Paris then deafened and dazzled. This was the time of Jean-Paul Sartre, Simone de Beauvoir, Boris Vian and Juliette Greco. Radio, cinema, and finally television enabled everyone to know what was going on all the time.

Yet Paris had hardly changed since the time of the Commune (1871), or since Baron Haussmann's reorganizations. Some years after the end of the Second World War, the consumer society exploded into being, and Charles de Gaulle (considered by many to have been the liberator of France in 1944) instituted the Fifth Republic in September 1958.

Despite the huge difficulties involved in the dissolution of the French colonial empire, the Ministry of Works in 1965 published an outline plan for the city of Paris in the year 2000. Vast building-sites sprang up everywhere, linked by an intricate network of transportation systems right across Paris and its suburbs.

The old market booths (*les halles*) were transferred to Rungis, a suburb to the south of Paris. For a number of years there was nothing but an enormous hole in the ground – until a new area of development, Les Halles, rose up from the earth together with the Georges Pompidou Centre of modern art (called the Beaubourg by the locals) in 1976.

It was thus in the second half of the 20th century that significant progress was made in improving the living conditions and the overall appearance of the capital. Renovation work then undertaken, including gigantic residential housing schemes (at Les Halles, Maine-Montparnasse and Bercy), virtually reshaped the capital and brought more of a balance between east and west. André Malraux, Minister for Cultural Affairs under President de Gaulle, decided to thoroughly refurbish Paris once and for all. His efforts towards sprucing the place up have lent the city a new lightness and cleanliness.

François Mitterand, elected President in May 1981, was a bit of a maniac for large-scale operations. Colossal expenditure was underwritten. Each new project presented special challenges in its accomplishment. The columns of Buren and the pyramid at the Louvre have since become very much part of the capital. But let's reserve judgement on the enormous cube that is the Grande Arche de la Défense (which is really nothing special, other than that it follows in the long line that also features the pyramid by the Tuileries, and the obelisk at the Place de la Concorde, the Champs Elysées and the triumphal arch of the Etoile). But we should also thank Mitterand for the renovation of the Louvre museum, which is now one of the greatest museums in the world.

The economic crisis that occurred in the 1990s slowed the frenetic pace of such operations. Most recently, the Museum of Asiatic Arts (the Guimet Museum) has just reopened after several years of closure. Due to open in 2004 is a new museum, the Musée des Arts Premiers, founded by President Jacques Chirac.

8- View of Paris with the cathedral of Notre-Dame, situated on the island of the Cité, and the Conciergerie.

9- The metro station Abbesses in the Art Nouveau style. The glass panel of this station has been perfectly conserved.

10- Renovation of the metropolitan train tracks near the Boulevard Saint-André, between 1900 and 1910.

Paris, capital of France, if anything, seems a little lost within the immense urban area that is Greater Paris. Every year it attracts millions of tourists from abroad who find in it much to enjoy and much to remember. The city really does cast a spell on those who come from afar and who like diving into history, but it certainly does not rely on tourists to survive. Yet it remains a particularly expensive place to live, and the population has been progressively decreasing (from three million in 1950 to two million now). It might seem to have lost something of itself with them, but look closely, and each of the current 80 *quartiers* of Paris has its own special spark of vitality.

From its first beginnings, Paris has renewed itself through constantly taking in new residents, first from the provinces, and later from farther afield.

Most radiant of cities, most mystical of cities, most romantic of cities with the Seine and its bridges … City of a thousand fantasies involving *les petites femmes de Pigalle* … Paris has many hidden corners and private hideaways unknown even to many Parisians.

Paris is essentially a place that mushroomed in the 19th century as a result of the Industrial Revolution. For the most part it is comparatively modern then, except for its historic core and the various traces of Gaullist and medieval times. It has never allowed itself to be entirely consumed by business interests. There are still some vestiges of Italian influence, of the Classical era, and of the century of the Enlightenment – when the whole of Europe spoke French. Such diverse influences still have a role to play in the 'art' of living in Paris. The Parisian woman stands out among others for her allure, her stylishness, her light-hearted ebullience and her spiritedly free speech.

Paris is likewise a free spirit, a breath of freedom blowing over it, with its rioting, its students' revolt of May 1968, its recurrent strikes. The city's very diversity makes it difficult to pin down.

Throughout the world, Paris represents style and luxurious elegance. It is the capital of *haute couture* (despite a certain amount of competition from across the Alps and across the Atlantic); it is in Paris that the best artisans – the ones from whom the *couturiers* constantly demand the impossible – live and work.

11- Jacques-Louis David, *Bonaparte crossing the Alps at the Mont Saint Bernard*, 1800-1801. Oil on canvas, 271 x 232 cm. National Museum of the Château de Malmaison, Rueil- Malmaison.

To discover the real Paris is not easy for a stranger to the city. There is just too much to see – museums, different areas of the city, and historical monuments. Be guided by your instincts. Take your time. Go places, stop and look at things, try to sense the special atmosphere of the capital. One life is simply too short to take it all in at once.

THE ÎLE DE LA CITÉ AND THE ÎLE SAINT-LOUIS

The Île de la Cité – once inhabited by the *Parisii*, then by the Romans – has from the beginning corresponded to the administrative, political, judicial and religious heart of the city. To a great extent that remains true today. Yet it is a great pity that Baron Haussmann was allowed to demolish bits and pieces even in this area. So there are now few traces left of the medieval period other than to the north of Notre-Dame. Every year millions of tourists trample all over its forecourt, on which no permanent building is permitted.

On the site of a temple to one of the Roman gods, during the first half of the 6th century, King Childebert I – son of the great Frankish King Clovis – built his own church, located slightly forward of today's cathedral. It was a tall church, later known as St Stephen's, its height witnessing to the power of the Merovingian rulers. During the 9th century it came under attack by the Normans. The contemporary Bishop of Paris, Maurice de Sully, then decided to construct a much bigger cathedral. Preliminary work began in 1163 and went on for 75 years. It was not actually completed until 1345. This was, after all, the great period of cathedral building. Notre-Dame became part of the history of France – but grew more and more dilapidated from the end of the 17th century. By the 18th it was in a dangerously unstable condition. Louis Philippe in the 19th century then undertook to restore it, trusting the work to Eugène Viollet-le-Duc.

The cathedral and its early Gothic style of architecture, is perhaps best seen from the Square Viviani on the Left Bank. Its solidity is imposing without being unduly massive. Flying buttresses (14th century) lend an impression of stability to the building as a whole.

The façade is represented by two high towers one each side of a central porch some two-thirds of their height. The three doorways are not symmetrical, as was often the case during the Middle Ages. The Gallery of the Kings of Judah and of Israel overhangs them. Above the central doorway – that of the Last Judgement – is a rose window dating from the 13th century. Higher still, an arched gallery adds lightness to this part of the frontage.

12- Notre-Dame, detail of the ironworks of the main entrance.

13- Notre-Dame, detail of the sculptures decorating the main entrance.

14- The façade of the Notre-Dame in spring.

The open forecourt of Notre-Dame affords a view of the west end of the building in its entirety – but that was not possible before Baron Haussmann's alterations, which cleared streets and houses in order to make it so. The centre of the forecourt is the point from which distances elsewhere are measured (usually in kilometres) from Paris.

The Rue de la Cité corresponds to part of the original north-south route in Gallo-Roman times. On one side now stands the main city hospital (the Hôtel-Dieu), on the other the Police Headquarters (the Prefecture) together with a flower- and bird-market.

This western side of the island is where the Roman authorities were stationed, and later where the Merovingian kings set themselves up within the protection of the Gallo-Roman embankment. The uprising led by Etienne Marcel caused King Charles V to hastily find himself somewhere else to reside, which he did in the Marais and at the Louvre. The royal palace later became the Parliamentary chambers, and then the Palais de Justice (the High Court). Buildings on the site have thus been modified many times over since the Roman era. In the 19th century Viollet-le-Duc restored and enlarged the palace. Nicely wrought iron railings (1785) lead into the cour de Mai (the May Courtyard).

15- Notre-Dame, seen from the courtyard.

16- Notre-Dame, architectural detail.

17- View of Paris with the Notre-Dame, the Pont de l'Archevêché and the Pont de la Tournelle in the south, and the Latin *quartier* in the west.

18- View of the Conciergerie and the Pont au Change.
19- The clock of the Conciergerie.

Hidden away from the outside world within the surrounding Palais de Justice is a treasure of glorious Gothic art: the Saint-Chapelle. King Louis IX, later canonized as St Louis, one way or another acquired possession of some priceless relics of Christ and determined to preserve them in a chapel he had specially built (1245–1248). Topped by a spire some 246 feet/75 metres high, the Sainte-Chapelle is a technological miracle of the Middle Ages, with its 48-feet-/15-metre-high stained-glass windows that have stood the test of time and emerged completely unscathed.

Right next to the Palais de Justice is the Conciergerie ('Caretaker's Lodge'). Built in Gothic style by King Philip the Fair in the 14th century, it was used as a prison during the Revolution to hold prisoners almost always awaiting execution on the guillotine. Queen Marie-Antoinette was incarcerated here while she too was under sentence of death. Its deepest dungeon was converted into a chapel of penance (precisely a 'penitentiary chapel') in 1816.

The square clock tower on the outside of this building, houses the first public clock in Paris. No one should ever leave the city without having seen it by night, without having gazed in admiration at the historically scenic panorama as the lights of the passenger-steamers on the river add to the other night lights, bathing all these monuments in their shafts of luminescence.

Just in front of the Cité, the Place Dauphine is an ancient royal square built by Henry IV. It leads on to the oldest bridge in Paris: the Pont-Neuf. Begun in 1578 under Henry III, the bridge was completed in 1604 by Henry IV, and was the first of its size not to have houses and shops on it, although it had pedestrian pavements on each side. It provides a highly convenient link between the Louvre and the Cité. At the middle of the bridge stands a statue of Henry IV wheeling his prancing horse to one side.

The Île Saint-Louis is connected to the Île de la Cité by a footbridge. It is not so bethronged with tourists as is its neighbouring island. Mind you, for centuries there was only rural countryside there, although the island was cut in two by a ditch dug right across it in the 14th century. It was as late as in the 17th century, following a reorganization of property rights, that the two islands became part of a single estate, and the Île Saint-Louis was itself split up into individual sites. Surrounded by high quaysides, it is well protected against the surges of the River Seine.

20- The Pont-Neuf.
21- A statue of Henri IV on the Pont-Neuf which links the island of the Cité and the VI *arrondissement*.

To take a walk on the Île Saint-Louis is quite delightful, with its serenely peaceful streets and its quaysides that afford spectacular views of the Left and Right Banks and of Notre-Dame cathedral. Many of the houses date from the 17th and 18th centuries, and there are several equally admirable *hôtels* (larger mansions that were once the town-houses of wealthy residents), including those of Lambert and Lauzun.

22- A rose window of the Sainte-Chapelle dating from the 13th century, and richly decorated frescos inspired by the Old and New Testaments.

23- The vault of the Sainte-Chapelle on the upper floor, which used to be reserved exclusively to the Royalty.

THE LEFT BANK

The River Seine winds fairly placidly from east to west through Paris, effectively cutting the city in two. There is a certain rivalry between the occupants of the two halves. Those Parisians who have made a deliberate choice to live on the Left Bank (the southerly bank) would sell their souls to the devil before transferring their allegiance to the Right Bank – and *vice versa*.

At the heart of the capital, the quaysides offer some excellent walks along the river – strolling, perhaps, in many places on the Left Bank, but at a more lively pace anywhere on the pedestrian pavements on either Bank. It is there that the dealers in second-hand books have their stalls, their books all arrayed in a multitude of boxes. Old books, posters, postcards, and antique prints are everywhere. The dealers have congregated here for nearly four hundred years. Threatened, but not disturbed, by Baron Haussmann's renovations, they have to this day doggedly continued to generate a good-natured hustle and bustle on the quaysides.

Downstream of the Cité, the Pont des Arts connects the Louvre with the Institut de France (the seat of the Academies of the Arts and Sciences). This bridge was constructed in 1803 for pedestrians only, but was replaced in 1982. From this spot there are magnificent views of the Île de la Cité and the surrounding terrain. Returning eastward, along the Quai de Conti and then the Quai des Grands Augustins (the oldest of all the Paris quays, built by Philip the Fair), the visitor comes to the Place Saint-Michel, which was established by Napoleon III. The Latin Quarter starts here, and stretches south to the slopes of the Montagne Sainte-Geneviève on which the Pantheon proudly stands, and west from there across the Boulevard Saint-Michel towards the Odéon.

This part of the Left Bank has been inhabited since the Roman era. There are still one or two traces of those times (the ruins of the Baths of Cluny, the Arènes de Lutèce in the Rue Monge). It was not until the 12th century that the schools and colleges were established, scattered at random, that would later be gathered together to form a university campus that enjoyed a high reputation across all of Europe. Latin was the official language in such places, and so the area became known as the Latin Quarter. The only true survivor from these illustrious medieval colleges is Sainte-Barbe – founded in 1460 and rebuilt in the 19th century – which, unhappily, was obliged to close its doors in 1999.

On its site atop the Montagne Sainte-Geneviève, the Pantheon – designed by Jacques-Germain Soufflot – was completed in 1790. Classical in style, its façade features a portico of Corinthian columns surmounted by a pediment sculpted by Pierre-Jean David. Initially a church, the Pantheon has since fulfilled many functions both sacred and profane; it is currently no more than a monument to famous Frenchmen.

24- View of the quaysides of the River Seine, a place of idle pleasures and long walks; the Parisians love to bask here in the summer sun.

25- A few kiosks on the embankments of the River Seine where one can buy newspapers, books, ancient engravings...

26- The Eiffel Tower, seen from the Palais de Chaillot.

Just around the corner from the Pantheon is the church of Saint-Etienne-du-Mont, which combines Gothic and Renaissance architectural styles. Close by is the church of St Genevieve, formerly a dependent church of the abbey of the same name. The saint's mortal remains were consumed by fire during the Revolution, but since the 19th century other relics have been housed in the church within a special reliquary. Saint-Etienne (St Stephen's) is, remarkably, the only church in Paris that still possesses a rood-screen (16th century).

Just behind Saint-Etienne, the gardens of the old Ecole Polytechnique (Polytechnic School) represent a little-known oasis of calm. The backstreets of this area are quite peaceful and charming too, if elderly — but that peace is rudely shattered by the frenzied traffic on the Rue Mouffetard (known as 'the Mouff') and the Place de la Contrescarpe.

A little farther off, the Jussieu Faculty of Sciences — built during the 1960s to replace the old Halle-aux-Vins (wine market) — is considered an excellent example of modern architecture. Curiously, the nearby Institute of the Arab World, founded in 1980 and ordinarily lumped together with the Jussieu Faculty, is instead regarded as a first-class model of harmony between modern architecture and Islamic art forms.

27- The St Michael Fountain, at the entrance of the Boulevard Saint-Michel in the V *arrondissement*. In its niche, St Michael, perched on a rock, is conquering the dragon.

28- Detail of the St Michael Fountain.

29- The Institut de France seen from the Louvre, linked by the Pont des Arts.

To the east of the Faculty, the Jardin des Plantes – with its very French style paths and walkways – is a botanical garden that dates from the 17th century. It has its own zoo and a natural history museum that earned an international reputation in the 19th century. The students' area also contains the Paris Mosque (built at the beginning of the 20th century), which displays examples of Islamic art and also enables a visitor to partake of a mint tea with Eastern pastries on its Moorish patio.

Coming down the western slopes of the Montagne Sainte-Geneviève, on the side of the Boulevard Saint-Michel, the visitor finds the beating heart of the Latin Quarter. In 1253 the university now generally known as the Sorbonne opened its lecture-halls to penniless students who wished to study theology. It was from this establishment that the first book printed and published in Paris was issued in 1470. Today, the Latin Quarter remains a favourite haunt of writers, editors, publishers and booksellers.

Pierre de Châlus, Abbot of Cluny, had a residential hall built in around 1330 right next to the ruins of the Roman baths. As seen today – and called the Hôtel de Cluny – the building is the one that replaced the original between 1485 and 1500, and exhibits a flamboyant Gothic style. Badly damaged during the Revolution, it was acquired in 1833 by Alexandre du Sommerard, who restored it and furnished it with carefully sought-out items from medieval and Renaissance times. Bequeathed to the nation at his death, it became a museum that opened to the public in 1844.

30- The Pantheon.
31- The Arènes de Lutèce.
32- The market on the Rue Mouffetard.

The *quartier* of Saint-Séverin is full of little streets of medieval charm – unhappily overrun by tourists. St Séverin's church displays different aspects of Gothic style. Close by is an old charnel-house (or mortuary crypt).

33- The Institute of the Arab World (Institut du Monde Arabe), designed by Jean Nouvel, with its architecture in two volumes (a parallelepiped and a curved mass, separated by a narrow gap).

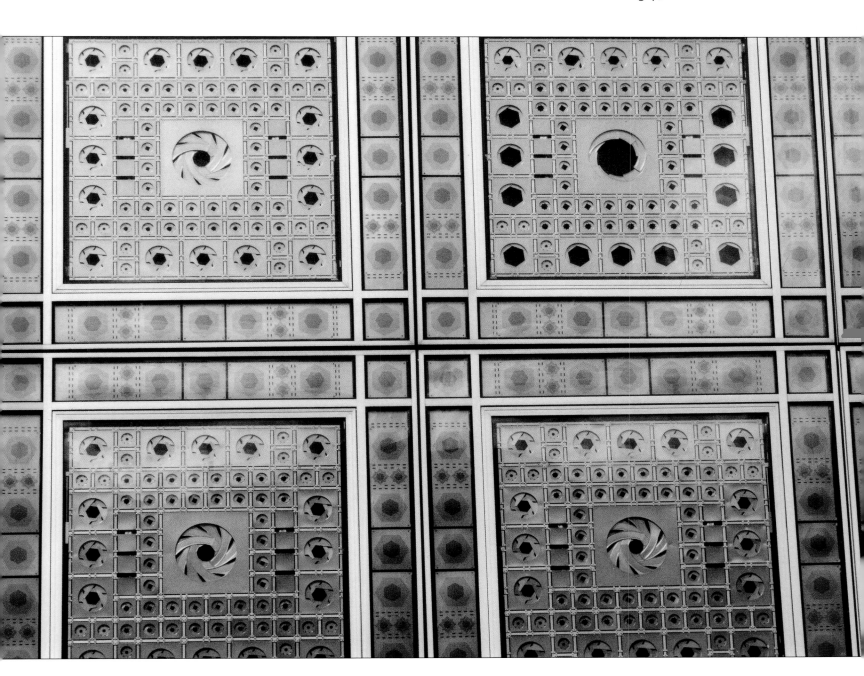

34- Detail of the façade of the Institute of the Arab World (Institut du Monde Arabe); the design of the diaphragms mimics Islamic ornaments. A computer controls their opening and closure in accordance with the sunlight's intensity.

35- The Grande Mosquée de Paris (Paris Mosque), seen from the main patio with a central marble basin inspired from the Alhambra of Grenada; the life of the mosque organizes itself around this area.

36- The interior of the Grande Mosquée, richly decorated with mosaics realized by Arabic artisans using two-millennium-old techniques.

37- Detail of a ceramic tile in the Grande Mosquée.

On the other side of the Boulevard Saint-Michel – the Odéon side – life, and traffic, is much more stimulating. To stroll down these streets during the evening is truly magical. Saint-Germain-des-Prés, as far as the Rue des Saints-Pères, is an area in which shops rub shoulders with cafés and restaurants. It has been a fashionable area in its time, especially just after the Second World War, thanks to its cafés, notably the *Flore* and the *Deux Magots*. The oldest restaurant is the *Procope*, and the most select in its clientele is the *Brasserie Lipp*.

It was in Saint-Germain that the skirmishes took place between rioting students and hard-pressed police in May 1968; Molotov cocktails and paving slabs from the Boulevard Saint-Germain against water-cannon, truncheons and riot-shields. Violence all round, featured on newsreels across the world. Many people in France thought the urban guerrilla had parachuted in to foment civil war, and that the wind of revolution was once again abroad in Paris.

Opposite the *Deux Magots*, the church of Saint-Germain-des-Prés is the oldest in the capital. Its foundations date from the 6th century. After attacks by the Normans, it was rebuilt at the end of the 10th century and at the beginning of the 12th, from which time the belltower remains, in ancient Classical style. The territory of the former Abbey of Saint-Germain – of which the church was a dependent benefice – extended over a huge area (amounting to no less than today's VI and VII *arrondissements*).

But is this *quartier* in danger of losing its soul? The booksellers and the publishers are under threat. Some have already gone. For the area is going up in the world. The little shops and boutiques have been taken over by prestigious giants like the *couturier* Armani and other great names in the world of fashion and luxury. The process is going on. At this rate Saint-Germain may become no more than an annexe to the Avenue Montaigne – although the atmosphere there is quite different. After all, Saint-Germain is on the Left Bank. And there are plenty of good-quality publishers still left, and antiques shops, and the last local cinemas to be found in the city.

38- The chapel of the Sorbonne, which was constructed in 1628 under Richelieu's command. It was annexed to the present-day Sorbonne university.

39- The cloister of the Church of Saint-Séverin made of limestone.

40- The interior of the Church of Saint-Séverin. The tinted glass windows were painted by Jean Bazaine and installed in 1970. This non-figurative art attempts to express the vitality of the spiritual world, of the invisible. The modernism of this art contrasts quite impressively with the architecture of the church, erected in the 15th century.

41- The *Deux Magots*, one of the key places of the existentialist movement, situated on the Place Saint-Germain-des-Prés.

42- The church of Saint-Germain-des-Prés, with its steeple dating back to the 11th century, which dominates the only belltower left standing after the invasions.

Another place well worth a visit is the School of Fine Arts (l'Ecole des Beaux-Arts) in the Rue Bonaparte, on the site of what used to be the Monastery of Augustinians Minor (le Couvent des Petits-Augustins). The church and the cloisters are still there. Directly opposite the Louvre, the Institut de France was founded through the generosity of Jules Mazarin, chief minister of France in the 1640s, who bequeathed his fortune to the building of a college. The statue of architect Louis Le Vau on the forecourt of the Louvre seems to look benignly across to the Institut, establishing a fine sense of harmony on both sides of the Seine. Today, the Institut is the seat of the Academies of the Arts and Sciences, including the Académie Française. In commemoration of his benefaction, Mazarin lies buried there.

To speak of the Quai d'Orsay is effectively to refer to the Ministry for Foreign Affairs, located next to the Bourbon Palace (Palais-Bourbon). The latter was built in the 18th century by Louis XIV's daughter, and originally comprised no more than a ground floor and a roof-terrace. It suffered some mischance during the Revolution, however, such that in 1807 modifications were felt necessary – notably to the façade – the main purpose of which was to create some visual harmony between it and the Magdalene church (l'église de la Madeleine) directly opposite. It now closely resembles an ancient Greek temple – and is the site of the National Assembly, in which the country's political representatives sit in parliament.

On the Quai Anatole-France, the Musée d'Orsay occupies an old railway depot built at the end of the 19th century and opened in 1900 to service the *Exposition universelle* of that year. When Giscard d'Estaing was President (1974–1981), it was decided to convert it into a museum of the 19th century. The museum is at a nicely intermediate point between the Louvre and the Pompidou Centre (le Beaubourg), and displays exhibits from the years 1848 to 1914. Many of them are works of art that have been donated by the Louvre, by the Museum du Jeu de Paume, by the Palais de Tokyo, and by various other benefactors.

At the western end of the Quai d'Orsay is the admirable Pont Alexandre-III, also built for the *Exposition universelle* of 1900. Immediately south (inland) of it is the Esplanade des Invalides, designed by Robert de Cotte between 1704 and 1720. The Esplanade leads in turn to the impressive Hôtel des Invalides, which of course has never been a hotel but rather a hospital and retirement home for soldiers. King Louis XIV noted that wounded French soldiers returning from wars abroad often had nowhere to live and no money to live on, and so created this establishment in 1670. It was constructed outside the city (as it was then) between 1671 and 1676, to the design of Libéral Bruant. Its church, Saint-Louis-des-Invalides, was completed a year later, designed by Jules Hardouin-Mansart who was also responsible for the church of the Dome, built between 1679 and 1706. The whole enterprise is all together a marvel of classic French architecture that bears witness to the grandeur and the magnificence of royal power as wielded by Louis XIV. It was restored under Napoleon III, and again in 1934.

43- Anglophone bookstores in the Latin Quarter, an intellectual turning plate in Paris.

The gilding was redone by command of President Mitterand at the end of the 20th century for the 200th anniversary of the Revolution. Ludovico Visconti designed Napoleon Bonaparte's tomb, placed inside the church of the Dome within its own circular crypt. The body of Napoleon – disinterred and brought back from St Helena – was formally buried there on April 3, 1861.

Not a stone's throw away, the Rodin Museum (formerly the Hôtel Biron) is not well known but has a beautiful garden. As an 18th-century *hôtel* it was taken over in the 19th century by the enclosed order of Sacré-Cœur. The sculptor Auguste Rodin then lived there from 1908 until his death in 1917. When the place finally became the property of the state, the decision was taken to make it a museum devoted to the sculptor.

Built between 1751 and 1772, the Military College (l'Ecole Militaire) was established by Louis XV to enable the sons of less wealthy aristocrats to receive the best military education. It was designed by the architect Ange-Jacques Gabriel. Napoleon Bonaparte attended the college, leaving it as a lieutenant in 1784, some years before it was closed by the Revolution. Today, the military still occupy the premises. From a distance, the Military College and the Hôtel des Invalides form a splendidly noble grouping together.

44- The Institut de France, siege of the immortals of the French Academy (Académie française).

45- The Assemblée nationale.

46- The Hôtel des Invalides.

47- The Pont Alexandre-III by night.

48- One of the four corner pillars of the Pont Alexandre-III, carrying a gold bronzed Pegasus. This particular sculpture, by E. Frémiet, represents the fame of the arts.

49- Auguste Renoir, *The Lady in the city*, 1883. Oil on canvas, 180 x 90cm. Orsay museum, Paris.

50- A candelabra, by H. Gauquic, of the Pont Alexandre-III, with sculpted loves wrapped around it.

51- Detail of the *Porte de l'Enfer* at the Rodin museum.

The main frontage of the Military College looks out onto the Champ-de-Mars, an old parade-ground sited by Gabriel on even older market-garden allotments. The Revolutionaries used the open space to celebrate the first anniversary of the storming of the Bastille on July 14, 1790. Other festivals of various kinds, military and civilian, have followed suit, such as the *Expositions universelles* of the 19th century, and that of 1937. It was at the beginning of the 20th century that the Champ-de-Mars was reorganized as a public park.

The Eiffel Tower is scenically situated beside the River Seine. A feature peculiar to the capital, it has become a symbol of Paris to the whole world. With the *Exposition universelle* approaching, engineer Gustave Eiffel in 1889 set about putting up a highly innovatory form of construction in little more than two years flat. It comprises a very light, very durable framework of wrought-iron trusses to a height of 986 feet/320 metres.

From the first, the Eiffel Tower had its detractors – and in some ways it is a wonder that the whole construction has not been dismantled. The most recent factor to save it was communications technology: a TV booster aerial was installed at the top, adding to its total height by some 66 feet/20 metres. A beacon at the highest point alerts night-flying aircrafts. Lighting the Tower at nighttime was completely rethought in 1987, however. Now it is magnificently lit during the hours of darkness, and in a way that perfectly illuminates its intricate lacework of supporting structures. In the mists of the morning, it stretches lazily, allowing only its sturdy feet to show.

Very close to the Latin Quarter is the Palais du Luxembourg, with its gardens. Queen Marie de Médicis – second wife to Henry IV – didn't like the Louvre and wanted to leave it. So in 1612 she purchased the Hôtel du Petit-Luxembourg and its surrounding grounds. Salomon de Brosse duly constructed a palace in the French style but with Italianate elements incorporated at the request of Marie de Médicis out of nostalgia for her native Florence. Renowned artist Peter Paul Rubens contributed to its decoration – the series of 24 canvases he painted for the queen is now in the Louvre. But the lady had scarcely installed herself in her new palace in 1625 when she was obliged to go into exile (1631), whereupon the building resumed much of its former name: the Palais du Luxembourg. During the Revolution it was used as a prison. With revisions by Jean-François Chalgrin and enlargements by Henri de Gisors, it is now the seat of the upper chamber of parliament, the Senate.

Its gardens – the Jardin de Luxembourg – are a haven of peaceful greenery within the capital particularly frequented by intellectuals. No one should miss out on seeing Salomon de Brosse's Médicis fountain, which depicts Acis and Galatea beneath a glowering Polyphemus.

South of the Jardin du Luxembourg (and the other side of a major road intersection), the Marco Polo gardens continue on to the Fountain of the Four Corners of the World designed by Gabriel Davioud (1873) and sculpted in bronze by Carpeaux and Frémiet, and then on to the Observatory Gardens (designed by Chalgrin). The Paris Observatory, founded in 1667, is still in operation today, but since the 1960s only as a centre for lectures and for complex data analysis, and as the headquarters of the International Time Bureau.

The modern military hospital in Paris (l'hôpital du Val-de-Grace) occupies yet another former ecclesiastical foundation. Anne of Austria made a vow that she would have a church built if she gave birth to a son to inherit the kingdom. Married for 23 years to Louis XIII, she finally brought forth the future Louis XIV in 1638. To fulfil her vow she entrusted the work to François Mansart. The church is in typical Jesuit style, modelled on the church of St Paul and St Louis in the Marais. Above it rises a dome that displays unusually ornate statuary. The abbot's chapel of St Louis connects with its outer passages.

A little to the west, an important complex of buildings begun at the start of the 1960s dominates the Boulevard du Montparnasse. Maine-Montparnasse is a strip of offices with a tower-block rising to 210 metres high containing 58 floors. However, the business centre of Paris, which has many such towers, is actually to the north-west of the capital, in the *quartier* of La Défense. Montparnasse in addition has many shops and leisure facilities. The station at Montparnasse, originally dating from 1848, has been entirely rebuilt in order to accommodate the modern rail traffic now increasingly vital. During the 20th century, Montparnasse was a *quartier* for commuters to work in within an otherwise rural environment. Achieving some celebrity because of the artists who migrated there from Montmartre, the area rapidly took on a fashionably chic air, kept alive by (among others) Pablo Picasso, Amedeo Modigliani and Moïse Kisling. Other contributors were Kiki de Montparnasse and Man Ray. Several artists' studios remain as they were. The smallish Bourdelle and Zadkine Museums make it possible for a visitor to imagine what the atmosphere in this *quartier* must once have been like.

As far south of the Paris Observatory as the Jardin du Luxembourg is north, lies the Parc Montsouris. It is a fairly recent creation (1867–1878) by Adolphe Alphand, who converted an area of unused land into an English style park very astutely using the natural slope of the terrain.

52, 54- Detail of the Fountain de Médicis with the characters of Theocritus' *Idyll.*

53- The Fountain de Médicis by Salomon de Brosse in the Jardin du Luxembourg; the artist reveals himself to be, with this particular creation, an inheritor of the Renaissance Mannerism.

55- The Palais du Luxembourg, built between 1615 and 1630, with its lines and symmetry announcing the French Classicism.

Next to the Parc several blind alleys, independent of time and oddly diverse in architecture, await the mildly curious walker. Likewise, on the other side of the Parc is the 'floral' part of the city, where the quiet little streets all have the names of flowers.

To the south-east of the capital is a zone that combines the last century with high-rise buildings. Renovations to the *quartier* have been for the better. The Italie-Choisy-Tolbiac area is an Asiatic enclave that preserves its own ways and customs. It is a lesser-known corner of Paris where it is possible to suddenly wonder if you are walking in a completely different country.

56- The Tour Montparnasse, 210m in height, is a 58 storey building with, on its 59th floor, Paris' highest terrace.

57- A shopping centre in the Chinese quarter of Tolbiac.

58- The Chinese New Year festivities.

59- The Parisian emblem, *Fluctuat nec mergitur*, on the gate of the Hôtel de Ville.

60- Detail of the Hôtel de Ville's clock with the inscription *Liberté, Egalité, Fraternité*.

61- Through a glass door of the Hôtel de Ville, we can see a spiral stair.

62- The Hôtel de Ville during summertime.

RIGHT BANK

Once the Left Bank had become well and truly occupied, it was the turn of the Right Bank to be developed. The area was less suited to it because the ancient river course of the Seine had left the ground very marshy.

The Île de la Cité is connected to the Right Bank by four bridges. One, the Pont au Change, leads to the Place du Châtelet. In medieval times this was a distinctly unhealthy place. Nonetheless, the civic authority of Paris really had its beginnings in the Parloir aux Bourgeois ('Council of Citizens') near the Châtelet. In 1357, Provost Etienne Marcel moved the council to the Maison-aux-Piliers on the Grève ('Strand') — to the site of today's Hôtel de Ville (City Hall). The Grève was so called right up until 1830, when it became the Place de l'Hôtel de Ville — now for some years a pedestrian precinct. Francis I had a much larger building constructed in Renaissance style. It was completed only during the reign of Henry IV. A major fire in May 1871 then razed the Hôtel de Ville to the ground. Rebuilt again to a design by Ballu and Deperthes between 1874 and 1882, the interior is sumptuously decorated.

Politically, the city of Paris has not always had one sole representative for it. Political power is after all vested in every one of its citizens. Mayors were elected by the citizens from the time of the French Revolution up to 1871, but it was not until 1977 that Paris had its next mayor, Jacques Chirac, later (in 1995) elected President of the Republic. As is visible everywhere in the capital, the State reserves its policing authority. For it has to be said that Paris has always been a place for insurrections, for the raising of barricades and for the incitement of mobs, all of which require forceful control.

On each side of the Place du Châtelet, two theatres were constructed to Gabriel Davioud's design in 1862. The St James Tower (la Tour Saint-Jacques) is the campanile of the 16th-century church of St James-la-Boucherie, destroyed not long after the Revolution.

To the east of the Châtelet, the Marais — which extends from the Seine to Turbigo, from the Boulevards to the Pompidou Centre — has its own special atmosphere. Several monasteries were located here in the 19th century, and began to bring the soil into agricultural use. King Charles V left his palace on the Île de la Cité and built the Hôtel Saint-Paul between the Rue Saint-Antoine and the Quai des Célestins. Nothing remains of it today. Charles VII installed himself at the Hôtel des Tournelles, which then became a royal residence. In 1559, during a jousting tournament at the Rue Saint-Antoine, Henry II fell mortally wounded. His widow, Catherine de Médicis, then had the Hôtel des Tournelles destroyed. Nothing now remains of that either.

In 1605, Henry IV decided, together with his chief minister, the Duc de Sully, to build a square of fine proportions to be known as the Place Royale, and to be surrounded by large town-houses all complying with strictly formal rules of architecture. The result was a stylishly elegant and homogeneous plaza visibly inspired by the French Renaissance. It was renamed the Place des Vosges in 1800.

63- The remaining ramparts of the Saint-Paul village.

64- A fountain situated near the lycée Charlemagne in the Saint-Paul village.

65- The statue of Joan of Arc.

66- An old sign near the Place Saint-Gervais, in the IV *arrondissement*.

There are quite a few large town-houses (*hôtels*) in the Marais, some noteworthy. The Hôtel Carnavalet, in the Rue de Sévigné, dates from the middle of the 15th century and was refurbished by François Mansart. The property of the city of Paris since 1866, it is now a museum devoted to the city's history.

Quite close to the Quai des Célestins, the Hôtel de Sens is — with the Hôtel de Cluny — the only actual evidence of medieval times still to be seen in Paris. Built at the end of the 15th century by the Archbishops of Sens (who at that time appointed the Bishops of Paris), it was for a couple of years the residence of the divorced and reputedly amoral Queen Margot (Marguerite de Valois), and later became a stage-coach terminal and transit office. The building was purchased by the city in 1916 in a very dilapidated condition. Now restored, it is the home of the Forney Library of the Decorative Arts.

The Hôtel de Sully was built in 1624 by Jean Androuet du Cerceau; it was then bought by the Duc de Sully, former minister under Henry IV (who had done so much for the Place des Vosges, at that stage known as the Place Royale). Particularly well restored, it is a notable example of 17th-century architecture. Today the Hôtel has become the International Center for Photographic Heritage, run by the Ministry of Culture.

After having had its moments of glory, the Marais experienced a definite decline. Its town-houses were no longer maintained, other buildings became run down. Formerly an area of artisans, it turned into one of the poorer *quartiers*. During the 1960s, Culture Minister André Malraux decided that it ought to be renovated. It has now been thoroughly cleaned up and is a delight to walk through. For a number of years it has also been the centre of the gay community. One or two authentic streets remain, such as the Rue des Rosiers and the Rue des Ecouffes (the mainly Jewish neighbourhood of the Marais).

The Bastille — perhaps the most potent symbol of the French Revolution — was built as a fortress by Charles V between 1370 and 1382. It was meant to protect the Hôtel Saint-Paul in which he was living, but became a prison for those who had offended the royalty either intentionally or unintentionally. A little before the events of the Revolution, such arbitrary imprisonments ceased. On July 14, 1789, when the Bastille was stormed by several hundred people beside themselves with revolutionary zeal, there were in fact a mere seven inmates still incarcerated. But the fortress, an emblem of royal power, was destroyed by the people of Paris. At its centre, the July Column (set up to commemorate the revolutionary events of July 1830) has on top of it the *Genius of Liberty*. It has become a major crossroads for cars travelling between the Faubourg Saint-Antoine, the Marais, and the République. Moreover, an ultra modern building by Carlos Ott — the Opéra Bastille, completed in 1989 — has replaced the old Bastille rail station. Despite some initial coughs and splutters, the Opéra Bastille seems now to have found its cruising speed.

To the west of the Marais, the *quartier* of Les Halles and Beaubourg has completely changed in appearance since the 1960s. At the beginning of the 12th century, a marketing centre for food of all kinds was established at Les Champeaux (the future *quartier* of Les Halles) because the market located at the Grève was no longer sufficient to feed the capital. Under the Second Empire, Victor Baltard and Félix Caillet constructed a number of gigantic pavilions mainly made of glass and metal — these were the famous Halles de Baltard, or just Les Halles (1854-1866). But with the rapid development of traffic on the roads came considerable logistical problems. In 1962 it was decided to move Les Halles to Rungis, a suburb to the south of Paris. Huge public outcry! But Baltard's pavilions were duly pulled down.

In 1969, President Georges Pompidou decided, for the benefit of the public, to create a modern cultural centre that would be available to all. A competition to design it was won by the architects Piano and Rogers, who envisioned a structure that caused no little comment. Nonetheless, the Pompidou Centre (known more often to the locals as the Beaubourg) since its inauguration in 1977 has received a multitude of visitors (and has recently reopened after some renovation and refurbishment). A commercial centre — the Forum des Halles — was built on the other side of the Boulevard Sébastopol. Pleasantly colourful gardens were created especially to brighten up this *quartier* otherwise sadly lacking in greenery. Around and about are ancient roads that go all the way back to medieval Paris. The Fountain of the Innocents, sculpted in Renaissance style by Jean Goujon in 1550, is a masterpiece. This is where the Cemetery of the

67- A richly crafted door.

68- The door of the Provencal restaurant "Aux Anysettiers du Roy", situated on the island of Saint-Louis. This restaurant was very popular in the 60's : Salvador Dali, Brigitte Bardot, Jerry Lewis and others were often seen there.

69- The Hôtel de Sully with its façades, witnesses of the Renaissance style.

70- The very modern Opéra Bastille is of an impressive size and can welcome 2700 spectators. It aspires to be a more open and popular opera.

Innocents used to be until it was demolished in 1780. By that time it was a veritable charnel-house from which emanated an appalling stench. All the bones were then dumped in the abandoned quarries that were themselves the remains of the catacombs of Denfert-Rochereau.

The church of St Eustache was built, from 1532, on the site of a medieval chapel. It has a Gothic floorplan not unlike that of the Notre-Dame cathedral, and is in addition Renaissance in style. The façade has, however, been reconstructed and has lost something of its original charm. Following a fire in the 19th century, Victor Baltard was commissioned to restore it.

The Rue de Rivoli runs across some of the Marais and straight past the Hôtel de Ville on its way to the Place de la Concorde. After the more commercial part of this road, the atmosphere changes as the road approaches the Palais-Royal (the 'Royal Palace'). On the right is the Louvre des Antiquaires, a sumptuous place one can walk into to take shelter from the elements. Opposite is the Louvre itself.

71- Detail of the Pompidou
Centre facing the Rue du
Renard; the centre has an
industrial style architecture
unique in the world with
its glass façade and
metallic structures
(staircases and blue, red
and green external tubes).

72- Near the Pompidou Centre;
aquatic sculptures by Nicky
de Saint-Phalle and
Tinguely.

73- The Forum des Halles with,
in the background, the
church of St Eustache
offering an interesting
contrast between classical
and modern architectures.

74- The Forum des Halles is the
only shopping and leisure
centre in the heart of Paris.

75- The Fountain of the
Innocents.

It was in 1200 that Philip Augustus — who at that time lived on the Île
de la Cité — built himself a fortress that would protect the royal treasures
while also serving as a prison. In the 14th century, Charles V made it
comfortable enough to live in without, however, taking up residence in it
himself. The cultural aspect to the Louvre's current vocation came about
through the establishing of the first royal library. The kings of France left
the Île de la Cité to live in the Marais, before they 'emigrated' altogether to
Touraine. The Louvre was virtually abandoned. In 1527, at the height of
the Renaissance, Francis I demolished the keep (the central stronghold),
putting the work of reconstruction in the hands of Pierre Lescot, and
committing the sculptural effects to Jean Goujon. Henry II and then Henry
III in turn approved of the way things were going. The south and west
wings of the courtyard square were duly built.

When Catherine de Médicis left the Tournelles, she decided to have
another palace built close to the Louvre. Philibert Delorme began
construction work in 1563, Jean Bullant took over in 1572. King Henry IV
recommended the programme in 1594, and the Flore and Marsan
pavillions were built.

The queen then requested a *passage* to be made for her to shelter in from
the elements when travelling between the Louvre and the Tuileries. The
Petite Galerie (1566) and the Galerie du Bord-de-l'Eau (1598-1608) duly
occupied the space. Later, Louis XIII enlarged the Louvre (the Clock Pavilion
and the extension to one wing were by Lemercier), and Louis XIV extended
the south wing and added north and east wings (by Le Vau).

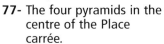

76- The Louvre seen from the jardin des Tuileries.

77- The four pyramids in the centre of the Place carrée.

All the various architects observed and respected the building style originally imposed by Pierre Lescot, with the result that the courtyard square is enclosed in remarkably homogeneous fashion. Finally in 1665, Louis XIV attempted to commission Gianlorenzo Bernini to build a splendid façade to the east front. But for once the famous architect and sculptor's plans were not up to standard, and it was instead Charles Perrault who designed the façade's colonnade and who completed the work on the north and south sides.

In the meantime, Louis XIV also made alterations to the hunting-lodges that had been built by Louis XIII at Versailles — alterations that would render the buildings worthy of himself as the Sun King. He moved in with his entourage in 1680. Work on the Louvre thereupon ground to

78- The Arc de Triomphe du Carrousel at the entrance of the jardin du Carrousel, annexed to the jardin des Tuileries.

79- The quad ridge on top of the Arc du Carrousel.

a halt, and was shortly afterward abandoned altogether. Squatters took over, comfortable in the knowledge that Louis XIV was preoccupied elsewhere, and at some distance. A century later, the Louvre was in a perilous state — but was rescued when, in 1789, Louis XVI bowed to popular demand and returned with the court to the Tuileries. Only to leave them once and for all on August 13, 1792.

Napoleon Bonaparte began building work again, on both the exterior and the interior. And on an enlarged Place du Carrousel he set up a triumphal arch (an *arc de triomphe*) in classical style to celebrate the achievements of his army (1808).

80- The Orangerie in the Tuileries.

81- A statue in the jardin des Tuileries.

82- Leonardo da Vinci, *Portrait of the Mona Lisa*, 1503-1506. Wood, 77 x 53cm. Louvre museum.

He was even allowed to ornament it with the quartet of bronze horses taken from outside St Mark's basilica in Venice (which had themselves been stolen by the Venitians during the takeover of Constantinople in 1204). But Napoleon was defeated, and the horses were returned to Venice. On the restoration of the monarchy, the sculptor Baron François Bosio replaced the quartet with another.

It was in the time of Napoleon III (ruled 1852-1870) that the Louvre finally took on the appearance it has today. But the Tuileries were burned down a year later, during the Commune. The Louvre was itself only just spared.

So the construction of the Louvre spanned several centuries, and the palace was progressively enriched with all kinds of internal and external decoration. It became a public museum in 1793, and the use of its enormous space thereafter to display the works of art 'imported' by Napoleon Bonaparte was highly significant — although of course that importation dropped off after the Emperor's downfall. During the 1980s, President Mitterand endeavoured to make it the greatest museum in the world, the 'Grand Louvre', which meant that the Ministry of Finances had to move out of the Richelieu Wing of the building.

The Chinese-born American architect I. M. Pei was brought in, and designed one large and three small glass pyramids that were set up in the Napoleon courtyard. In 1989 —the 200th anniversary of the Revolution — the Pyramid was ceremonially instituted. Reviled at the time, it now seems quite appropriate. At nighttime the scene is captivatingly beautiful. From the Pyramid a spiral staircase leads to a basement section and into the museum through a vast and airily light hall.

The Louvre has thus been greatly altered over the past few years, in fact since the activities of de Gaulle's minister, André Malraux. Displayed inside are antiquities from the east, and from the classical periods of Egypt, Greece, Etruria and Rome; works of art dating from the Middle Ages to the first half of the 19th century; paintings from the 18th to 19th century, and sculptures; and contemporary and historical exhibits relating to the Louvre itself. This museum therefore represents a true success-story as much for the French as for people of foreign lands. Hundreds of thousands come every year to admire Leonardo da Vinci's *Mona Lisa* (*La Gioconda*), Veronese's *The Wedding at Cana*, the *Venus de Milo* (properly, the *Aphrodite of Melos*), the *Winged Victory of Samothrace*, the *Seated Scribe* (le *Scribe accroupi*), and other great works of art. Schools of painting exhibited include French, Italian, Spanish, and those of the Nordic countries. To visit the Louvre properly requires a good deal more time than a single day.

83- *The kiss* by Rodin, bronze, at the Orangerie of the Tuileries.

84- The obelisk of the Place de la Concorde.

85- Detail of the obelisk.

The Louvre and the Palace of the Tuileries together once made a spectacular group. The Tuileries is no longer there ; only its gardens remain —and from them it is possible to look out over exceptional views of the Place de la Concorde, the Champs Elysées, the triumphal arch of the Etoile and, farther away, La Défense. The gardens of the Tuileries, between the Place du Carrousel and the Place de la Concorde, are today typical of French public gardens in that they are arranged with order and symmetry. Catherine de Médicis initially turned land growing wild into a park of the Italian style, with fountains, grottoes and wild animals, and so forth. She made it a pleasant place to walk in. Louis XIV's highly influential minister Colbert then (in 1664) asked landscaper André Le Nôtre to change the look of the gardens. He created the Terrace of the Feuillants to the north, and the Terrace of the Bord-de-l'Eau to the south. It is the path down the middle that affords a unique prospect. The gardens were then opened to the public — and their popularity was such that seats were made available for hire. A bit later, the Regent Philip Il, Duc d'Orléans, diverted such enjoyment in a more dubious direction: the gardens at nightfalll became the scene of debauchery. In June 1794 the Festival of the Supreme Being (which celebrated the Revolution's return to religious doctrines) took place here, and extended over onto the Champ-de-Mars.

Today, the gardens of the Tuileries preserve much of the aspect that Le Nôtre meant them to have. Many statues greet the visitor's gaze, including some by the sculptors Antoine Coysevox, Nicholas and Guillaume Coustou, and Aristide Maillol.

At the very end of the gardens of the Tuileries is the Musée du Jeu du Paume — built by Napoleon III — at which short-term exhibitions are often held. The Musée de l'Orangerie, on the other hand, contains the *Nymphéas* by Claude Monet, together with many works by the Paris School (Picasso, Modigliani, Utrillo, Renoir, Cézanne, and others).

The Place de la Concorde — a truly immense open space — is gloriously illuminated at night. On marshy land belonging to Louis XV, architect Ange-Jacques Gabriel created an octagonal 'square' in homage to the king. An equestrian statue was commissioned from Edmé Bouchardon and Jean-Baptiste Pigalle. At one end of this Place Louis-XV, Gabriel erected two impressive buildings: on the right was the Maritime Ministry, while the left housed, among other things, the sumptuously appointed Hôtel de Crillon. Altogether the construction took twenty years (1755—1775). In 1792, however, the statue of Louis XV was taken down, and the site became the Place de la Révolution — on which stood the guillotine. Louis XVI succumbed to its blade on January 21, 1793, followed by more than a thousand other victims, including Queen Marie-Antoinette on October 16 of the same year.

86- Detail of the fountain on the Place de la Concorde.

87- The obelisk on the Place de la Concorde and the Eiffel Tower.

88- The Magdalene church.

Executions continued in this fashion until 1795. Finally, under the form of a Revolutionary government known as the Directory (1795—1799), the site was given its current name of the Place de la Concorde.

In the middle of it is the ancient Egyptian obelisk taken from the ruins of the temple at Luxor and presented to Charles X in 1829. It was set there only in 1836. On the side of the Place next to the Champs Elysées is a copy of the statuary ensemble known as *The Horses of Marly* (by Guillaume Coustou), while on the Tuileries side is a copy of *The Winged Horses* (by Antoine Coysevox). At the corners, mounted on plinths, are statues representing eight great cities of France, by Ange-Jacques Gabriel.

Between the two old private royal residences, the Rue Royale (1732) leads to the church of St Mary Magdalene (the Magdalene church, known in French as *la Madeleine*). In the Rue Royale, Maxim's Restaurant (1890) was celebrated during the very early years of the 20th century for the various beautiful courtesans who used to frequent it.

The Magdalene church looks much like a Greco-Roman temple. Work on it began in 1764, and the church was finally consecrated in 1842. Without a belltower or a cross on top, it has a unique nave and is surmounted by three cupolas. It is framed, on all sides, by a colonnade. Above the peristyle at the front is a frieze by Philippe Lemaire representing the Last Judgement. The building is lent even more classical *gravitas* by a flight of 30 steps up to the entrance.

Once the Place Louis-XV had been established, a bridge was built across the river to link it with the National Assembly. The bridge in time became known as the Pont de la Concorde and, ironically, was constructed partly of the rubble remaining from the destruction of the Bastille.

From the Place de la Concorde, a stretch of greenery extends to the circular open space (the Rond-Point) almost halfway down the Champs Elysées. It was in 1667 that the landscaper Le Nôtre took charge of the area to the west of what was then Paris. It included the gardens of the Champs Elysées, among which were located several theatres and luxurious restaurants.

The *Exposition universelle* (World's Fair) of 1900 left behind it a number of buildings that were not necessarily intended to remain. Minor exhibitions have occasionally been held in the Grand Palais, which was made almost entirely of metal and glass. However, the place became so run down that it was decided to close it to the public until it had been completely restored. Joined to the Grand Palais, the Palais de la Découverte – built in 1937 – is renown for its Planetarium. The Petit Palais meanwhile, which is also undergoing refurbishment, contains collections of works of art belonging to the city of Paris. The whole assembly of buildings may be impressive and suggestive of the Baroque, but it is neither historically accurate nor particularly French in style.

89- A statue on the roof of the Grand Palais.

90- View of the Champs Elysées and the Arc de Triomphe.

91- Detail of the Arc de Triomphe.

92- A metro station.

93- The columns, designed by Daniel Buren, in front of the Palais-Royal.

94- The mobile steel sculptures by Pol Bury.

The Champs Elysées is considered by many to be the most beautiful avenue in the world. When it had all its gardens, up till 1724, it used to climb the mildly sloping Chaillot, the future Place de l'Etoile. But the avenue became progressively urbanized during the 19th century – a place for the fashionable to see and be seen while out walking – before becoming thoroughly democratized in the 20th century. Yet it is still a highly prestigious area, and has recently been slightly reorganized. Every year on Bastille Day, July 14, a formal procession descends down the Champs from the Etoile to the Place de la Concorde – and it is here that the city of Paris celebrates its Liberation. For the Champs is itself a symbol known all over the world. It was here that the national French soccer team came following their stunning victories in the European Cup and then the World Cup, amid indescribably enthusiastic scenes of joy.

Each side of the Champs are areas redolent of both business and money. This part of the VIII *arrondissement* has many esoteric boutiques and art galleries. The streets of the Faubourg Saint-Honoré (in which the Palais de l'Elysée – the presidential palace – stands), the Avenue Montaigne, the Rue François I, and so on, are much quieter than the Champs Elysées. This is where French *haute couture* has for many years now had its headquarters, trailing in its wake no few Italians and Americans.

Monceau Park, an old hunting estate of the Dukes of Orléans, is today a garden in the English style, and well maintained, as is appropriate to this residential area. During the 18th century, Carmontelle worked out the initial plans, allowing his imagination something of a free rein. The project then was abandoned for a time, only to be resurrected when the Péreire family of bankers bought up one part of the land, leaving Baron Haussmann's collaborator Alphand to turn the rest into the parkland it now is.

At the top of the Avenue des Champs Elysées, the Place Charles-de-Gaulle-Etoile (from which no fewer than twelve beautiful avenues branch out in all directions) is based on a mound that no longer exists. The Arc de Triomphe was set up here, designed by Chalgrin to the order of Napoleon in honour of his victorious army. Work on it was completed during the reign of Louis Philippe. The Place with its avenues was the work of Baron Haussmann. All around the Place, the buildings present identical façades, thanks to Hittorff (in 1854). On November 11, 1920, the body of an Unknown Soldier killed in the battle for Verdun in the 1914–18 Great War was buried at the foot of the monument. Every evening a commemorative flame is lit to the memory of all the soldiers who have died for France. This classical style triumphal arch is much larger than the one on the Place du Carrousel. On the side that faces the Champs Elysées, Rude's *La Marsellaise* is a masterpiece. Sculptors Etex and Cortot also contributed excellent work to the monument.

95- The Place Vendôme.

96- Detail of the column on the Place Vendôme.

Outside the old Paris city walls but reached following the continuation of the Avenue des Champs Elysées (across the Pont de Neuilly, a bridge which spans yet another looping arm of the Seine), is the *quartier* of La Défense. This *quartier* into being with the establishment of the National Centre for Industry and Technology (Centre National des Industries et Techniques, or CNIT) 40 years ago, which generated the construction of many high-rise buildings around it. It is the big business centre of Paris – the equivalent of Manhattan in New York, or the City in London.

Returning towards the Arc de Triomphe at the Etoile, it is rewarding to make a little detour by the Place du Trocadéro, in the direction of the Eiffel Tower. On this rather higher area, Catherine de Médicis had a country house built. Later it became a monastery. Napoleon tore that down, meaning to put up a palace there, but his intentions came to nothing as he ran out of time. Yet in 1878 a palace was built there, and then for the *Exposition universelle* of 1937 a much larger and better palace was constructed – the Palais de Chaillot. It is a modern building built to a symmetrical design comprising two 'pavilions' each of which has a wing that curves outward and away, separated by a courtyard that looks down on the Champ-de-Mars and the Military College. This courtyard — the Parvis des Droits de l'Homme ('Courtyard of the Rights of Man') – is very often completely overrun with sightseers, some of whom undoubtedly have the glint of battle in their eyes. The Palais de Chaillot is home to the Maritime Museum, the Museum of Humankind, the Museum of French Monuments, the National Theatre de Chaillot, and a movie/film library-collection. Its gardens meander down to the Seine, and tourists may take their leisure on the banks, looking back to see the fountains play.

A stone's throw away stands the Guimet Museum, probably the most important museum of Asiatic arts in the world. It has recently reopened after five years of closure.

The Palais de Chaillot is otherwise surrounded by an area of residential housing – fashionable, expensive, and quite modern. Wealthy Parisians would formely go on vacation in the villages of Passy and Auteuil, just outside the old city walls to the west. They still have a certain charm. A number of building operations have been undertaken on properties in this XVI *arrondissement*. In about 1900, artist and architect Hector Guimard began to construct houses and buildings in the style he especially favoured – Art Nouveau – partly in reaction to Baron Haussmann's rigorous conformism.

In the old 'village' of Auteuil, the suburban villas, the careful grouping of houses, and the odd blind roads all bear witness to the love of the inhabitants for a discreet way of life, so 'far away' from the madding crowds of the city centre.

97- The Palais Garnier, the theatre of the Paris Opera, was built in the fastidious style of the Second Empire. It was to replace the opera on the Rue Le Peletier, destroyed in a fire in 1871.

98- A statue on the dome of the Paris Opera.

99- The statue representing choreography on the rooftop of the Paris Opera.

Farther west still lies the Bois de Boulogne, a haven of peace for Parisians between Neuilly and Boulogne, two inner suburbs of the capital. The ancient Forest of Rouvray, reserved for the Royal Hunt, used to be very much larger than the area of the Bois ('Woods') today. First reshaped by Colbert, who drove roads straight through it, it was later despoiled by Allied (Anglo-Prussian) occupationary forces who encamped in it after the Battle of Waterloo in 1815.

It was much later that Napoleon III entrusted to Baron Haussmann and to Alphand the task of transforming this forested landscape into a park in the English style, with lakes and waterfalls and winding paths. Not far away are the race-courses of Auteuil and Longchamp. The Bois de Boulogne suffered considerably in the great storm of December 26, 1999. In places, the area was so devastated as to be almost unrecognizable.

During the late 1630s, Cardinal Richelieu bought up some land at the back of the Louvre. It already had a large residence on it, but he pulled it down, meaning to develop the property. Architect Jacques Lemercier was brought in to build a new mansion, the result being the Palais-Cardinal. Foreseeing his death, however, Richelieu bequeathed the palace to King Louis XIII – who himself died several months later, in 1642. Anne of Austria then lived in it with her son, the future Louis XIV, and for a time the Palais-Cardinal was the royal residence (le Palais-Royal).

100- The Vivienne galerie.
101- A bookstore in the Vivienne galerie.
102- The Jouffroy passage.
103- The Grévin museum.

Political unrest thereafter caused the king to reside instead at Saint-Germain-en-Laye, and to decide he would never return to the Palais-Royal – which he gave to his brother Philip, Duc d'Orléans. The place took on a much less savoury role when the dissolute and debauched duke became Prince Regent.

104- The Moulin Rouge is one of the most famous music halls of Paris. It opened its doors on October 6th, 1889. Its creators, Joseph Oller and Charles Zidler, referred to it as the first Palace of women and hoped that it would become the most grandiose temple dedicated to music and dance.

It is difficult to imagine the Palais-Royal so crowded with people as it must have been during the 18th century. Today, the French style gardens provide a peaceful and elegant setting. Having lost general favour, it has become popular once more. The Council of State, the Ministry of Culture and various other state organizations now occupy the premises.

In the main forecourt stand the pillars put up by Daniel Buren in 1985–1986, in black and white marble, of differing heights, on the surface of what used to be the carpark. They are not as visually interesting, perhaps, as the mobile steel sculptures of Pol Bury. Indeed, Buren has been heavily criticized.

105- The Porte Saint-Martin.

106- The basilica of the Sacré Cœur.

Close to the Palais-Royal is the circular Place des Victoires, an old 'square' built in honour of Louis XIV. It was Marshal de la Feuillade who in 1685 commissioned a statue of His Majesty, and requested Jules Hardouin-Mansart to construct a classic regimental parade-ground around it. During the Revolution, however, the statue was melted down. The statue there today is by Bosio (1822).

The other royal square created in Louis XIV's honour is the Place Vendôme, built in memory of the Duc de Vendôme, son of Henry IV. Louvois, Royal Superintendent of Works, intended to produce a square more beautiful than the Place des Victoires (1686) – but his disappearance halted the work, which did not resume again until 1698. Mansart then devised a wide, octagonal space surrounded by elegant frontages. In the middle was an equestrian statue of Louis XIV by Girardon. It suffered the same fate as did the statue on the Place des Victoires. In 1810, Napoleon erected a column there, together with cannons captured at Austerlitz. For a time, statues were put up and were removed one after another. Finally, the Emperor himself came to look out over the Place Vendôme.

The area was the cradle of French *haute couture*, which has since mostly transferred across towards the Avenue Montaigne. But Patou and Chanel remained faithful to this quartier. Coco Chanel used to rent her apartment at the Ritz by the year. Refurbished some years ago, it is one of the wealthier zones of the capital, the headquarters of many jewellers.

In 1860, one Charles Garnier won a prize for designing a grand opera-house. Fifteen years later, in 1875, the Paris Opera was inaugurated. Garnier's building was impressive (if not even oppressively impressive), and of a style described as Napoleon III. The outer façade was decorated with a great number of sculptures, including *La Danse* by Carpeaux.

The Magdalene church marks the starting-point of the Grands Boulevards. This is another commercial area, containing large stores and cafes which appeared mostly during the second half of the 19th century and attracted a fairly prestigious clientele. The opening of these large stores is one of the reasons for the disaffection for the Parisian *passages* (see below) that is still felt today.

The wooden *galeries* of the Palais-Royal, built in 1786 by Victor Louis for the Duc d'Orléans, achieved no small success – before they were destroyed in 1828. Sheltered from the elements, their gambling-parlours and brothels made for a very lively scene, for such well-appointed dens of vice attracted crowds of punters. The later Galerie d'Orléans, which succeeded them, built in stone, was far less highly regarded. The return to accepted morality in the Palais-Royal meant the disappearance from there of its former commercial enterprises.

The Revolution changed the mindset of Parisians. A new, prosperous *bourgeoisie* emerged, and speculation in real estate greatly intensified. The streets in Paris were dirt-covered and had no lighting. It was at that stage, on the Right Bank, that covered *passages* – the pavement arcades – were introduced, which afforded shelter from the elements, and were lit by natural light during the daytime and by gas mantles at night. Such *passages* effectively comprised gentle short-cuts between two fast-

107- The dome of the basilica of the Sacré Cœur.
108- The Montmartre mound and its funicular.
109- One of the Moris fountains offered to the city of Paris at the end of the 19th century.
110- A living sculpture in Montmartre.

flowing streams, each side of an 'island' of houses, connecting it with the many shops lined up along both sides. The *passages* were extremely popular, yet enabled a person to stroll at leisure and in peace – although the theatres and the nearby literary *salons* might occasionally and abruptly deluge them with feverish activity.

More popular than the *galeries*, these arcades were something especially Parisian in the 19th century, and an original idea that was quickly adopted by much of the rest of Europe. Yet only the *passages* in Paris have ever possessed such intimacy, such charm, such a mystique – quite different from the rather showy imitations to be seen in London, Milan, Naples and Berlin. Most of them were built during the first half of the 19th century. Baron Haussmann's renovations, the arrival of rail transport (which caused the ultimate decline of long-distance couriers), and finally the larger stores and shops all seriously affected the popular use of the *passages*. They have now all but gone forever – although some people still hope they will make a recovery. There are a mere twenty of them still left today.

111- The village of Montmartre.

112- A series of old publicity posters.

Each *passage* or *galerie* has an atmosphere that is all its own – and that deserves special attention. Véro-Dodat, recently restored, is a *galerie* that holds much to admire. Vivienne is indeed vividly animated, while its competitor Colbert, with its delightful rotunda, is more elegant yet seems to lack the prosperity it has evidently been expecting. The *passages* on the Boulevards (Panoramas, Jouffroy, etc.) are not so elegant but are more lively. Others (such as Caire and Brady) are focuses of what we might today call professionally physical activity: these are the *passages* that are least well cared for – indeed, often downright dirty.

At the beginning of the 20th century, *galeries* were built along the Champs Elysées, but possessed nothing at all of the spirit of *galeries* of the 19th century. Meanwhile, the modern galerie of the Place du Carrousel of the Louvre is a contemporary adaptation of the old *passages*, with natural lighting courtesy of the Pyramid.

In 1784, a wall was built all around the city of Paris at the behest of the Farmers-General (the taxation officials). Currently, an orbital freeway follows most of the line of that wall. The Boulevard de Clichy and the Boulevard de Rochechouart form the borders of the old 'village' of Montmartre, annexed to Paris in 1860. Below the slopes, Clichy and

Pigalle have an international reputation for nighttime pleasures involving women of little or no virtue. This is the area of the capital with the greatest concentration of sex shops and 'escort girls'.

Montmartre has a high reputation with tourists, and, of course, on top of its hillside, also features the basilica of the Sacré-Cœur (the 'Sacred Heart'). It was here that St Denis was beheaded during the 3rd century. In fact, the name Montmartre undoubtedly derives from *le Mont des Martyrs*, and one of its main streets, the Rue des Abbesses, likewise bears witness to the presence of an ancient convent. It was in the 18th century that the land began to be parcelled out into lots. Because the earth has through the centuries been so thoroughly dug over, the hillside is fragile, and architects and builders have to be very careful about where they put new housing. Recently, the upper area of the Rue des Martyrs experienced serious subsidence.

Montmartre quickly drew to itself artists and writers who appreciated the peculiar charm of its steep and winding streets. Its many stairways lend the *quartier* a special attraction that is increased tenfold at night when all is quiet and deserted. The painters who used to live hereabouts led raffishly bohemian lives – before they migrated on to Montparnasse at the beginning of the 20th century.

113- The artists' meeting place on the Place du Tertre.

114- The Port de Plaisance in Paris.

But apart from that quietness in the 'village', which persists to this day, it has to be admitted that the true icon of Montmartre is the Sacré-Cœur. After the disruption of 1870, the basilica was the beneficiary of national subscription. Abadie commenced work on it in 1876, and the work went on – under the authority of others – for almost 50 more years. The basilica was consecrated in 1919. Completed in Romano-Byzantine style, its massive white exterior can be seen from a great distance. The inside is richly decorated.

In front of the basilica, the *terrasse* of the Sacré-Cœur is like a hanging garden above the rest of the city. Paris thus lies at the feet of anyone who takes the trouble to stop there for a few moments.

Right next to the extremely popular basilica is the much lesser-known church of Saint-Pierre-de-Montmartre. It is actually one of the oldest churches in Paris (12th century). Although altered and rebuilt, it incorporates four marble columns that were once part of the structure of the Roman temple situated on the hilltop, and the oldest ogive arches in the city.

Also in Montmartre is the Place du Tertre – peaceful in the mornings but thronged with tourists in the afternoons. Art students there make sketches of them at amazing speed. How many of them are aware, though, that on the hilltop every autumn, the grape harvest from several vines is celebrated, or that Montmartre has many little-known corners, thousands of nooks and crannies unknown to the gawping crowds?

Richer residents live in 'villages' to the east of Paris, generally outside the old city wall of the Farmers-General. From 1802, Napoleon decided to create a network of canals that would not only improve the transportation of freight around the capital but supply drinking-water too. The canals of the Ourcq, St Denis and St Martin, and the canal Bassin de la Villette, were all built at the beginning of the 19th century, and have constituted essential arteries important also to the economic sector. Recently, the banks of the canals have been upgraded to afford pleasant walking. A pleasure-boat centre – the Arsenal – is located between the Bastille and the River Seine.

115, 116- The vines in Montmartre. The grape harvest around Paris dates back to the Gallo-roman period. During the Middle Ages, the wine in Montmartre, produced under the direction of the abbesses, had a very good reputation. In the beginning of the 1930s Pierre Labric, mayor of the independent commune of Montmartre, decided to replant a vine. Every year, the vintage is given an original name evoking the cultural and historical events of this *quartier*.

117- The celebration of the grape harvest with its queen and the exaltation of the vintage spirit of Montmartre. These festivities occur each year on the first Saturday of the month of October.

118- The brotherhood of the Montmartre Republic during the parade of the celebration of the grape harvest. Its members wear Aristide Bruant's costume. This brotherhood came to exist in 1921 with the intention of perpetuating the Montmartre tradition and spirit. Its slogan is "doing good with joy".

119- The City of Science and Industry is one of the biggest scientific and technical centres in the world as well as one of the most innovative. Adrien Fainsilber is its architect. The City welcomes 3.5 million visitors every year.

The Parc de la Villette, crossed by the canal of the Ourcq, now stands on the site of abbatoirs that were renovated at huge expense but for no purpose at all. It was a terrible scandal. In the first years of the 1980s, however, a City of Science and Industry was designed, including an enormous spherical public arena (unlike any other in France or in the world), the Geode, the equally vast Zenith Hall and the Great Hall, which houses *salons* and exhibitions of various kinds, and the City of Music (the architect Portzamparc). Also on the plans of the Parc as drawn up by Bernard Tschumi are around ten areas of park gardens.

This sector of Paris has been subject to property speculation that has been both anarchic and highly political in social terms. Residential accommodation there is intended for the working-class population. Over thirty years or so, the area has changed and has benefited from what have become known as President Mitterand's Great Works – an endeavour to bring the east of Paris up to the general standards of the west.

To the south of the Parc de la Villette is another park, Buttes-Chaumont – built on top of some old quarries – that is known to few Parisians. As with Montsouris and the Bois de Boulogne, it was Napoleon III (and his landscaper Alphand) who designed this park with its cliffs, its boulders, its waterfall and its lake. It is distinctly a place that is off the beaten track, in the capital, but well worth discovering – like some of the little streets farther out in the east, with their villas and odd blind roads.

At the time of Louis XVI it became necessary to prohibit the burial of any more corpses in the already full to stinking cemeteries around the city churches. Public health was suffering. So new cemeteries had to be established outside the city walls, on land acquired by the city of Paris, in 1803. One of these was the cemetery of Père-Lachaise, now renowned for the hundreds of famous people buried there. It was the landscaper Brongniart who was commissioned to shape it in such a fashion that it would be possible also to stroll pleasurably through it.

Mitterand made his mark in the south-east of Paris, and on both sides of the River Seine. The Ministry of Finances moved from the Louvre and took up its brand new headquarters at Bercy. The surrounding parkland is modern and adjoins the old wine warehouses on the Right Bank of the river. Some of it has recently acquired little shops that are open on weekends only.

France's National Library – the Bibliothèque Nationale de France, François Mitterand – on the Left Bank opposite the Bercy parkland, corresponds to President Mitterand's desire to give access to knowledge to the widest possible public, and to give some relief to the overburdened former National Library in the Rue de Richelieu. The latter is actually an old royal library built by Mazarin and was greatly improved during the 19th century by Labrouste.

The Bois de Vincennes is a large green open area in the east of the capital. For a long time from the Middle Ages, it was – like the Bois de Boulogne – an old Royal Hunting Forest. It has benefited from royal attention ever since, notably when, following the construction there of a hunting-lodge, a castle was built. When Louis XIV took up residence at Versailles, he did not forget Vincennes. But it was in fact Napoleon III who ordered Alphand to create the Bois as it is now. From the time of the Colonial Exhibition in 1931, there also remain the Museum of African and Oceanian Art, the International Buddhist Institute, and the zoological gardens.

120- The Geode.

On the outskirts of Paris, the flea markets are a speciality of the capital. Hundreds of stalls set out in neatish rows every weekend sell second-hand goods of all descriptions, mostly household stuff like clothes and personal items. The flea market of Saint-Ouen is the most popular. Friday is the day reserved for the professionals. After them come the privateers. The bedlam round some of the second-hand stalls contrasts with the decorum of the neighbouring booksellers' stalls. It is not unlike a Middle-Eastern *souk* – and you may find it just as important to know how to haggle there. The area is one in which the over-formal, over-authoritarian aspects that the city has picked up over the last couple of decades may be left behind for a few hours.

EPILOGUE

Paris – the metropolis visited by more people than anywhere else in the world – has over the centuries thus become a city whose influence has spread across all of Europe, indeed across the whole world. And in spite of rivalries both political and commercial from medieval times to the present, Paris has always been a focus for those who seek culture, those who seek knowledge, and those who seek personal freedoms.

But those who succumb to the charm of Paris are without number, whether they come here to stay, rapt forever, or to be here for just one more day and one more day and one more day . . .

121- The Défense.

Chronological table

52 B.C.
The Romans conquered Lutèce, a small village of fishermen (les *Parisii*).

360.
Julian (331-363) was proclaimed Roman emperor in the Lutèce arenas.

486.
Clovis (around 466-511), king of France from 481 to 511, chose this city as capital. Hence, Lutèce continued its expansion, notably on a religious level. However, she was abandoned by the following kings, including Charlemagne, and threatened by the Norman's raids in the 9th century.

987.
After the accession of the Capetian dynasty, Paris became once again the capital of the kingdom and knew an urban expansion as well as a considerable economical development.

1163.
Maurice de Sully started the construction of the cathedral of Notre-Dame.

13th century.
Paris was the most popular city of the Christian Occident with its 100 000 inhabitants.

1348.
The epidemic of the plague killed about 25 000 people.

1429.
Joan of Arc attempted to liberate the city of Paris, which had made a pact with the English during the 100 Year War, a conflict that opposed France and England between 1337 and 1453.

1572.
Saint-Bartholomew massacre decimated the Protestant Parisian population during the bloody night of the August 23rd to 24th. More than 3 000 people died. This massacre was on the order of King Charles IX, advised by his mother Marie de Médicis.

1594.
Henry of Navarre, a protestant, abjured his faith and became Henri IV, king of France. The Louvre was his main residence. The new king looked after the improvement of the city: establishment of the Place des Vosges, of the Place Dauphine, of the embankments of the Arsenal, of the Clock...

1610.
Louis XIII, son of Henry IV, came to the throne. The city continued to expand with the development of new quarters (the Marais, the Faubourg Saint-Honoré and the Bastille).

1634.
A new wall was built. It was situated where the boulevards from the Bastille to the Magdalene are now located.

August 26th, 1648.
The day of the barricades during which the people rose up to ask for the liberation of Broussel, consultant in the Parisian Parliament, arrested following Anna of Austria's demand. He was opposed to the government's measures. This event marked the beginning of the Fronde, troubles that shook both Paris and France. This civil war was fomented by the parliamentarians, and then by the nobility. They contested the absolute monarchy and Mazarin's government during Louis XIV's minority. The young king and his mother, Anna of Austria, were forced to leave the Louvre and take refuge in Saint-Germain-en-Laye.

1652.
The Fronde ended, Louis XIV and Anna of Austria returned to Paris where they received a triumphal welcoming. The royal power came out of this confrontation even stronger.

1680.
Louis XIV left Paris to settle in Versailles. However, the city remained the siege of the Parliament and the administrative capital. Furthermore, it was under his reign that were erected, under Colbert's authority, the colonnades of the Louvre, the Invalides, the Salpêtrière, the Institut de France, the Portes de Saint-Denis and de Saint-Martin, the Places Vendôme, the Place du Carrousel, the Place des Victoires...

1784.
Preceding the Revolution, Paris had a population of 650 000 inside the city toll, that was to be the city's frame until 1860.

July 14th, 1789.
The taking of the Bastille by the people. This fortress was a prison, symbol of the absolute monarchy's despotism. This was the beginning of the French Revolution. Paris became once again the centre of France.

1806.
The emperor Napoleon I strived to make Paris capital of Europe. He organized great building projects (the *arcs de triomphe*, the colonne Vendôme), accelerated the equipment of the city (establishment of markets and abattoirs, opening of the Ourcq canal, supplying of drinking water, sewerage system...) These developments accompanied by certain esthetic improvements (such as the construction of the Magdalene and the Pantheon) were continued during the Restoration (1814, return of the monarchy after Napoleon's abdication) and the July Monarchy (the given name of the reign of Louis-Philippe I - see below).

July 27th-29th, 1830.
The July Revolution, also known as the "Trois Glorieuses". It was an insurrection against the reign of Charles X and his government who had cancelled the elections, modified the electoral system and abolished the freedom of press. The opposition first burst out among the workers in the publishing industry and the

students, and then spread quite rapidly. The Parisian rebels went towards the Hôtel de Ville, the Louvre and the Tuileries. Victorious, they asked for the establishment of a Republic but the deputies proposed the solution of order and appeal to the Orléans family. Charles X abdicated in favour of his grandson by accepting to nominate the Duc of Orléans as lieutenant general and regent of the kingdom.

1841- 1845.
The fortification of the Thiers forming a belt around Paris, situated where are now located the Grands Boulevards.

February 22nd-24th, 1848.
Days of insurrection that put an end to the July Monarchy, which was replaced by the 2nd Republic, proclaimed on February 25th, after the invasion of the Palais Bourbon.

December 2nd, 1851.
Coup d'Etat by Louis-Napoleon Bonaparte, president of the 2nd Republic, who was able to eliminate the legislative assembly and reinforce, to his benefit, the executive power. The new constitution (January 1852) prepared the advent of the Second Empire.

December 2nd, 1852.
The reestablishment of the Empire up until 1870 by Napoleon III. It is during this period that, under the supervision of the Baron Haussmann, Paris transformed into its modern appearance. Napoleon reinforced the administrative, economical, social and cultural centralisation. Paris lived through considerable change, characterized by a concern for visionary urbanism as well as political preoccupations.

1871.
Paris experienced a surge of demographic growth (1 800 000 inhabitants).

March-May 1871.
The Parisian commune. A revolutionary government was formed to fight against the Prussian domination. This government began with the military occupation of Paris.

1878, 1889 and 1900.
The *Expositions universelles* (World's Fairs) took place in Paris, proof of its growth and prosperity. The Eiffel Tower was erected during the 1889 fair.

1914-1918.
The First World War during which Paris experienced both bombings and aerial raids. After the war, Paris began to expand its geographic boundaries on the entire department of the Seine.

1934.
Political and social feverish excesses were known throughout Paris and shook the public opinion, which brought about right-wing manifestations.

1936.
The retort of the workers', political parties emerged onto the creation of the Front populaire (a left-wing political party).

1939-1945.
The Second World War: Paris' occupation by the Wehrmacht that begun in June 1940. The dark period of the Occupation was marked by the deportation of many Jews and other minorities, by the actions of the Résistance... The city was liberated on August 24th, 1944. On the 26th, the French troops led by the general de Gaulle, walked down the Champs-Elysées.

September 28th, 1958.
The new constitution was approved by referendum and inaugurated the 5th Republic.

1958-1969.
General de Gaulle's presidency.

May 1968.
Economic, social, political and cultural crisis. The contentious movement started in the universities of Nanterre and of the Sorbonne. They led to the riots and barricades in the Latin *quartier* where the students confronted the police. The movement won over the working class. A general strike followed these events, which paralysed the country.

1969-1974.
George Pompidou's presidency.

1974-1981.
Valéry Giscard d'Estaing's presidency.

1981-1995.
François Mitterand's presidency. During his two seven-year term of office, he undertook great renovations in Paris that modified its architectural landscape: the Bibliothèque Nationale François Mitterrand, the pyramids of the Louvre, the arch of the Défense...

1995.
Jacques Chirac was elected president of the Republic.

1998.
Paris was the host city of the World Cup, which was won by the French soccer team, provoking an astonishing effervescence in the streets of Paris.

2004.
Paris will welcome the *Exposition universelle* (World's Fair). Its theme is the image.